Once there was a beautiful tree with thousands and thousands of multi-colored leaves that shimmered in the sun and whispered in the wind.

Most of the leaves lived a simple life.
They unfurled from small buds, opened
to their full size, dried up and fell to the
ground where they eventually became
the soil needed by the tree to grow.

A few rare leaves learned how to break from the tree before drying up. They sailed on the wind to pools and puddles where they would drink to stay alive.

One such leaf was many hues of purple and was very proud because he had broken from the tree during a storm when he was young and strong.

He hid this pride as he told stories of his adventures because he wanted to make other leaves feel good so that they would tell him where the nearest water places could be found.

"Oh my sleek-skinned friends, do you know that my very body has been lifted great distances and placed near pools of water so large that I thought they had no end? Do you know that I once had to lay my stem carefully at a pool's edge so that I would not over drink or become lost in its depths? I have seen creatures that never leave these waters and move as if they are flying through the air. With a single wiggle they move like a lightning bolt. Oh the things I have seen…"

Over time, the purple leaf became very good at dazzling his fellow leaves with his wonderful stories. They were flattered to be his "sleek-skinned friends" and would even share the water inside themselves in order to keep the purple leaf with them. To share water was to give away a portion of life and though it was painful, the leaves gave their water freely because the stories made them feel so full of life.

The purple leaf no longer needed to search for water, he only needed to find other leaves, and this allowed him to travel much more freely.

It felt so good to be free and to have so few limitations that the purple leaf flitted quickly from leaf to leaf and stayed just long enough to earn the trusted bit of water. Soon he could convince a fellow leaf to share its water with him happily in only a short time and his travels were even longer and stories even more exciting and glorious.

As time passed, the purple leaf noticed that something was souring inside him. He was impatient and angry if other leaves talked too long or didn't realize that he was a busy traveler who couldn't wait around for silly little tree-bound stories.

He noticed that it was hard for him to stay near a pool of water and wait for the wind to lift him out because it felt so limiting.

He noticed that when he told leaves he would come back with more stories, he rarely did. He avoided familiar spots and preferred new ones that might be more interesting.

Thep urple leaf was changing color and getting darker by the day. His veins were large and heavy from the quick and deep drinks he would take from other leaves as soon as they gave permission. He didn't lift in the wind like he used to. He was growing patches that were brownish-black colored and decided it was time for a change.

There were rumors of leaves who had learned how to reattach to a tree in order to be healed from sicknesses and he became obsessed with this possibility. He gathered together all the possible tricks and ideas, found a good-looking tree, and attempted to make the connection.

It was very frustrating for him.

Despite the fact that he would sharpen his stem and find a nice soft branch to burrow into as the wind pressed him into the trunk, he fell out after every attempt. He didn't want to be stuck to a tree again and an old leaf told him that this was what held him back

He tried to focus on all the good times he'd experienced as a young leaf as he tried again and again to burrow in. After many failures, he realized that he was dying. His color was now mostly brown and his veins were constricting so much he doubted much water would go in.

He began to worry that all he had learned would be lost and realized that he had actually shared very little of his life with any other leaf. All his stories were told to get water, but there were deeper questions and lessons he had gained through his adventures which he had never spoken.

Finally he began to fall. As he landed on the soft ground and he felt the worms began to crawl upon him, he began to weep out the last little bits of water still left in him. "What a waste!," he thought. "I have been given so much and it has been used for so little. I am sorry for all the leaves who gave me so much of themselves and for my tree that I left without a thought of thanks for the life I was given.

At least I will feed these worms," and his body was chewed down to the stem and finally down to nothing.

The previously purple leaf could think no more.

There was only darkness where there had once been life.

Some time later…

A bud opened on that same tree. It unfurled slowly and felt scared of the cold wind and the bright sun. As it was pushed open by the flowing sap from inside the trunk, it had memories come into it which were surprising.

The tale of the purple leaf had come through many roots and entered the bud in a sudden flow. It was shocking but also thrilling to have the memories of another life come into it and slowly feel as if they were its own experiences. As it felt the purple leaf's sorrows, a tiny tear formed at the tip of the bud and fell to the earth below.

The bud saw so many memories and felt so many emotions. So many experiences rushing into it caused it to begin to see the world as a vast and beautiful adventure. As it looked at the connection between the earth, the tree, the air, and the sky it wondered, "Am I made of the same things that cause the night sky to be dark and the stars to be so bright. Am I a part of things that are so enormous? Could my little life be a part of such greatness?"

As it marveled at this, it also knew that it would not spend its life as the purple leaf had. It felt wrong to have something so wonderful trapped in the body of one leaf. Any water the bud received, it would use to spread life to many. It would one day become a full sized leaf and would share its color and gentle movements in the breeze so that the world would be brighter and more full.

The little bud felt warm with the hope that the good inside of it would some day show the way toward wonders yet to come.

The Tale of the Purple Leaf

Copyright © 2022 by Eric J. Epstein, Photography by Ron Sweetin, all rights reserved. No part of this publication may be reproduced, stored in a retrieval system or transmitted in any form or by any means (electronic, mechanical, photocopying, recording or otherwise) without prior written permission of the author.

cover and interior design by Nathan Schiro

ISBN: 978-1-7350318-2-8
Printed in the United States of America

www.ingramcontent.com/pod-product-compliance
Lightning Source LLC
Chambersburg PA
CBHW041217070526
44583CB00001B/15